1 MONTH OF
FREE
READING

at
www.ForgottenBooks.com

By purchasing this book you are eligible for one month membership to ForgottenBooks.com, giving you unlimited access to our entire collection of over 1,000,000 titles via our web site and mobile apps.

To claim your free month visit:

www.forgottenbooks.com/free153135

ISBN 978-0-484-41022-9
PIBN 10153135

CATAWBA RIVER,

AND

OTHER POEMS.

BY

JOHN STEINFORT KIDNEY.

New-York:

PUBLISHED BY BAKER AND SCRIBNER,

No 145 Nassau Street, and 36 Park Row.

1847.

CATAWBA RIVER,

AND

OTHER POEMS.

BY

JOHN STEINFORT KIDNEY.

New-York:

PUBLISHED BY BAKER AND SCRIBNER,

No 145 Nassau Street, and 36 Park Row.

1847.

Entered according to the Act of Congress, in the year 1847, by

JOHN STEINFORT KIDNEY,

In the Clerk's Office of the District Court for the Southern District of New York.

E. O. JENKINS, PRINTER,
114 Nassan Street.

TO

JOSIAH COLLINS, ESQ.

OF

SOMERSET PLACE, LAKE SCUPPERNONG,

NORTH CAROLINA,

This Volume of Poems

IS RESPECTFULLY AND AFFECTIONATELY

DEDICATED.

CONTENTS.

~~~~~~

CATAWBA RIVER.

With oaken pillars yonder height is strong,
  To which the bristling pines are clambering.
Beneath—Catawba frets, and speeds along :—
  The softened roar is asking me to sing :
    And, river! thou shalt move this day
    Through this, I think, thy virgin lay.

II.

While wintry showers were falling yesterday,
  The little pines were bent with dismal grief;
With faces buried in the snow they lay :
  But this strong wind has given to them relief ;
    And, dark within the world of white,
    They make it more intensely bright.

1

III.

Crowning the distance pure, the mountains lie,
  Now full of glory in the rising morn :
In those cool summits basking in the sky
  Like shining clouds, O river ! thou art born ;
    And frost is busy in the dell
    From which thy feeble waters well.

IV.

But let me roll away this winter dress,
  And hush the madness of the driving air ;
And show thee in thy summer loveliness,
  When happy breezes rove about thee there :—
    For Fancy shivers—*now* to seek
    Thy birth-place in the snow-clad peak.

V.

A rocky palace in eternal shade,
  All wildly roofed with tufts of brightest green,
With sweetest moss, and gleaming flowers inlaid,
  —Its grim and native terror all unseen—
    Rises, within the forest, high ;
    A veil of leaves its only sky.

VI.

And at its foot still tenderer is the moss :
　　The flowers creep down in huddling ranks around,
And fairy odors all about they toss ;
　　Cradling in beauty thus that faintest sound
　　　　Thy gurgling voice all softly makes,
　　　　When first the darkness it forsakes.

VII.

O, in that nest woven with gentle hues
　　Thy trembling life all feebly is begun :—
Child of the sunny showers and nightly dews !
　　From such a home thy devious race thou'lt run ;
　　　　Like all things else upon the earth,
　　　　The purest at thy place of birth.

VIII.

In powerless loveliness thou seemest to lay,
　　Like many a darling one—so softly moving :
Unable yet with any joy to play,
　　Yet all the fitter for the gazer's loving :
　　　　Untaught, as yet a little while,
　　　　Conscious of happy life, to smile.

IX.

Now sleeping half the time beneath the grass,
    Then, rounded to a pool, gemming the green:
Thus anxiously thy sober life doth pass;
    Still sadly beautiful where thou art seen:
      As yet in many doubts immured,
      Whether thy being is assured.

X.

But, nourished by the unneglectful sky,
    And by the bubbling rills that from beneath
Steal to thy bosom ever silently,
    And to thy strengthening life their own bequeath,
      Soon does thy life its fullness feel,
      Its power delighting to reveal.

XI.

Loving and joyous with thy crowding hopes,
    Thou'rt pressing closely now thy loving banks;
Then with still rapture sliding o'er the slopes;
    Now murmuring softly thy content and thanks;
      Then with a gleam of foamy white,
      Laughing in keenness of delight.

XII.

And soon thou art a lovely brook, revealing
  Within thy broader depths a leafy bower;
With over thee the matchless odors stealing
  From damask and the gold azalia's flower;
    While white and purple lilies seem
    Over their images to dream.

XIII.

The silent deer about thee come to drink,
  Where'er the mossy sward slopes from the hills:
And through the steeper banks thy waters sink,
  T' embrace in gloom the tributary rills
    That die for joy to reach the home
    Whither they've spent their life to come.

XIV.

In thy rich fringe that casts unbroken shade
  The breeze is lost,—and cannot come to play
On thy pure bosom whither it had strayed;
  And 'mid the rustling reeds it sighs away:
    But thou. beneath that sadder voice,
    Makest thine own the more rejoice.

1*

XV.

From this thy darkest, calmest home of all,
    At length thou leapest to the open sight,
Still where the shadows of the mountains fall :
    Athwart whose sombre sides, like fluttering light,
        The crimson birds, and birds of blue,
        Do glance the solemn verdure through.

XVI.

'Tis there thou seest first the azure sky,
    —A greater grandeur than aught yet to thee:
There first thou lookest to the mountains high,
    —The gorgeous land of thy sweet infancy :
        Yet nothing loath to move along ;
        In thy new freedom proud and strong.

XVII.

And, curving round the brown and rocky steeps,
    Thou hurriest to the sweetly opening dale :
There first above thee too the willow weeps ;
    And there thy wavelets rise to greet the gale ;
        And thither, to some grassy cove,
        The sturdy water-birds will rove.

XVIII.

Through fruitful valleys next thou wilt resound:
  There all about thee, fair plantations sleep,
Pent in by sober forests all around,
    Alive with feeding herds, and snowy sheep;
      And living voices cheerly ring
      To thee a human welcoming.

XIX.

Such art thou *here*—now quiet in the woods,
  And now in rapids roaring to the fields;—
Now curling round the rocks in hissing floods;
    And now the lowland smoother passage yields:
      A river proud and turbulent;
      In many a curve and angle bent.

XX.

O, I have watched thee on a summer's night
  Catching the moon upon thy glittering spray;
Circling the gloomy rocks with foaming light;
    Sending the silver mist through woods away;
      And where 'mong islands calm thou rolled,
      Beating their sides with liquid gold.

XXI.

And when thy distance-softened rushing floats,
  Fading, and swelling,—in its midnight moan,—
To gentler sounds, and all the shriller notes,
  It is the low and solemn undertone;
    Making a blessed harmony
    To rise beneath the hollow sky.

XXII.

Yon nook may give a hint to fancy too,
  —Where branches droop with such protecting
      grace—
To note the outline of a dark canoe,
  Where lurketh one of that departed race
    That once about thee wandered free,
    And, river! gave a name to thee.

XXIII.

And on for many a mile, such art thou still;
  Only with sister rivers greater grown:
Urging thy passage with unerring skill,
  To make the home of waters too thine own;
    And ever with a rapture tost,
    To be in its deep bosom lost.

Thy course is calmer far in yonder land—
   Where dismal woods and dark morasses be ;
Where not a pebble rolls upon thy strand,
   And earth is level as the waveless sea ;
    Where hangs the graceful jessamine
    In wreaths of gold, the woods within.

XXV.

There, in the gloomy swamps the black pools lie,*
   Studded with ranks of feathery cypress trees ;
Which thither wading from the cheerful sky,
   And from th' uneasy presence of the breeze,
    Seem pillars to the halls of Death ;
    Where never stirs a living breath.

---

* I may hope to have pictured to those who *have* seen, and scarcely to those who have *not*, this entirely unique feature in the scenery of the swampy region of the South. These perfect and motionless mirrors, thronged with singular cypresses, give an impression of their own, which is more like that produced by looking at a picture or a statue, than any other I know of in nature.

XXVI.

And in the shining pond, each cone-like base
  Seems resting on its image from below ;—
The slim trunks shooting toward heaven's brighter
    face ;
    Whose other selves down into darkness go;
      And all is, like a picture, still :—
      Fixed thus, beneath the Master's will.

XXVII.

There too the forest roof is hung in gray,
  The dusky emblem of a mourning land ;
With long moss trailing down from every spray ;—
    Like funeral weeds sent from the Maker's hand
      To mark the terror of the place,
      And warn our all too venturous race.

XXVIII.

Through such a land, O river ! dost thou roll,
  The ocean's sandy shores at length to lave :
Thy arrowy force, beneath the vast control
    Put back subdued, subsides into its grave.
      There wilt thou take unquiet rest,
      Diffused throughout thy mother's breast.

XXIX.

For thou art born—whene'er the living sun
His cloudy messengers with vapor fills:
—Life ever ending, yet again begun—
Should they be wafted to thy native hills,
And the dry earth shall drink the rain,
To feed thy feeble spring again.

SUNRISE AMONG THE MOUNTAINS.

THE sullen darkness slowly moves away
From the cool peak, and slumber from the brain.
Far o'er the west the night is rushing on :—
She sweeps in beauty o'er one half the world,
Kindling the lights of heaven where'er she goes,
Bearing their splendor through her dim domain.
Yet, in the zenith, watcheth one bright star,
The last and lingering angel of the gloom,
Once purely resting in its cold blue home ;
Now—slowly sinking through the warmer light
That up the eastern sky how softly springs !
Farewell, O night !—and thou, O seraph star,
Blest guardian of the twilight morn, thy reign
Resigning to the lawful king—farewell !

And hail, dawn of the rising day!—I wait
Thus high upon the mountain top, alone
Amid the crags, and in the thin, gray air.
Silence hath lain her finger on the earth,
Awhile, before the goings on of heaven;
And motion sleeps upon the distance vast,
Now nothing but a wilderness of clouds
That weigh in countless masses on the sight.
To the far sky the gentle billows fade;
And near me, surges break upon the rocks;
And here and there, a spray-attended wave,
Upreared above the rest, seems rolling on
With ruin in its bosom;—yet all still,
And fixed in one tremendous sleep!—As though
All winds that blow, let loose at once, had torn
The agonizèd ocean into foam;
And then both wave, and foam, and spray were *fixed*—
With frost omnipotent forever fixed—
Its fiercest life fixed in a solemn death!
And all the boundless sea is pale,—or clad
In sad and corpse-like hues.—So might have seemed
The richest plain the Torrid Zone doth bear,

2

—Gorgeous in velvet hills and forests dark—
When some drear, pestilential blight had come
And sickened every lovely tint to death,
And melted all to its own poison hue.

But see—the heaven is ready for the sun !
The East begins to smile at his approach,
And spread her rosy signals through the sky ;
And Joy is clustering round the blessed place;
And shouts are there, that mortals cannot hear !
The purple beams still chase the pearly light
Up to the higher ether.—Mount, O mount,
Ye crimson heralds of your glorious King,—
Stream ye your richness through the yielding blue !—

Am I alone—to see the monarch come ?
No heart but mine to tremble with the air,
—The crimson air—that trembles round his path ?
And none but mine to feel the joyous pang
That needs must pierce the all-too-earnest breast,
When the full vision fills the eye of faith ?
O painful privilege !—would *one* could share !

—And there the clouds *do* burst, and one black form
Uprises swiftly on the ambient !—
Welcome, bold bird !—I'm proud to gaze with thee.
Thou too a monarch, worthy art to see
Thy monarch come, when else to all the world
He draws this misty veil to hide his face.
Soar on, with moveless wing, through upper sky ;—
Soar on—my eye delights to follow thee,
Familiar as thou seemest, child of earth !

Lo now, that ruby spark upon the clouds !
That for an instant twinkles like a star,
—A mighty star, with light unborrowed proud—
And now expires upon a fair, round arch,
That glides like music on the listening sense !
—Yet not a *sound !*—no strain as sweet as life—
No dreamy tones with softest pulses moving
Through the deep tranquil heaven all along,
Comes to the painèd air !—But while I look,
I feel the music living with my life—
Yea,—filling all the hollow of my soul,
And centering there in one melodious orb

As big with bliss as yonder floating world!
Awake, creatures of breathing life, awake!
Thou sleeping earth, awake!—the day is born!

The cloudy ocean kindles with the light.
High-heaving wave, and deep and gloomy gulph,
And hanging spray, are brightening as it falls,
And glances onward to the western realms;
And death is cheerful with the show of life.
Still higher lifts the King his burning eye,
Till all the distance glows beneath his glance.
No more the sombre, saddening hues—but now,
Are softest clouds in gentle sleep reposing,
Sunk in their own embrace, and dazzling white
As after summer showers, as drifts of snow
Piled fresh and pure within an endless sea.
O, so the Sun of Righteousness arose
—While music rang along the vault of heaven—
Upon a world sick with the taint of sin,
And shed his beams of life to heal the woe.
The sun has bid the clouds away at length,
That he may shine upon the patient earth.

A faint commotion quivers through the mass;
And parting, blending, it begins to move.
They rise around me—solemn, grand, and slow,
And breaking in a thousand lazy forms,
With all the tardiness of majesty,
They wander upward to their own blue home.
They go to hang within the hollow sky,
As beautiful as any dream of heaven.
Ye splendid things! how soft and mild ye seem!
But yet I know ye are the homes of power.
With all your gentle, holy innocence,
Ye are the prisons of a thousand storms
Shall rend and horrify the blessed earth.
O well I know the thunder sleeps with you,
And the dread lightning coils within your breast.
The tempest winds are nestling closely now;
But they will scatter all your fleeces far;—
Aye, they will mock the silence that ye keep,
And send their wildly-screaming voices forth
To cheer the lightning to his awful aim!
To howl their fury in the deep ravines,

And fright their echoes from the trembling rocks—
—The echoes that must ever be unheard!

Pass on—pass on—mount through the willing air!
Farewell, ye brightest, darkest things, farewell!
I see the emerald robe of earth again,
Girt with its silver threads,—I love it more
Than yon light fleece the gale doth blow away.
There is a cheerful singing in the ear
That tells the work of life is going on.
Welcome!—thou dear, warm world—of grief and
      love!

SONNETS.

OF woman's life yours is the fairest time,
Ye blooming girls! As in a budding rose,
Whose early red gives promise of its prime,
Hope dwells the sweet unfolding life within,
And Beauty with each ray more beauteous grows;
Thus, in you dwelling, they the gazer win.
How innocence is mingled with the blush
Of riper girlhood!—How the bursting gush
Of transport is subdued beneath the sense
Of maiden modesty!—and no pretence,
—Such as in after years may find a place—
Of what ye do not feel, doth mar your grace;

As yet unconscious of the anxious thought

Which with another year may to your hearts be
  brought.   .

II.

Glide on, ye beings of the deep-hued cheek,

Of heavy, clustering curls, and beaming eyes!

—Those eyes which to the gazer are so meek,

And mild like the full moon; yet no surprise

Should e'er be felt, to see them warm and bright,

And lively as a meteor in the night—

So gentle, yet so frolicksome and wild,

While o'er the woman reigneth yet the child.

O happy lot!—if, in these early days,

Before an anxious thought for future fate

Upon your griefless hearts full heavy weighs,

To feel the birth of Love ye might not wait—

If Love, just budding now, through life should .
  flower—

O, that were woman's destiny in Eden's bower!

Could this be true—then would *my* heart again
At Beauty's altar droop, in love's sweet pain.
For when, O brightest One ! the time shall come
For *thee* to feel a fluttering at the heart ;
When the first rosy leaf shall burst its home,
Laden with fragrance from the inner part ;
Could I be there to catch the odorous blush—
To drink from out thine eyes the primal gush
Of tenderness ; and could the passion bloom
Unchecked by age, and through the days of gloom ;
That were the old intended Paradise !—
Does a true vision now my heart entice ?
Or doth the tasked imagination weave
A woof unreal,—that the heart may grieve ?

IV.

TO THE SAME.

[WRITTEN TWO OR THREE YEARS AFTER.]

O MAIDENS,—with a dear, poetic thought,
I loved you once :—that love I must gainsay.
The stealing months no cheerful change have wrought,

But taken something lovely quite away,

I fondly hoped, the child might on be brought,

Enveloped in the woman still to stay.

Your modesty had such a beauteous fear:

Nor did your girlish boldness it destroy :—

But now, too bold,—and now, unseemly coy

Ye seem, ungraceful yet in newer sphere.

Ye rosy ones, your beauty still I see—

But yet it kindles not a warmth in me;

—That warmth which made you lovely in my song—

Now in these plainer numbers must ye move along.

[WRITTEN SOME YEARS LATER.]

But lo !—the rose is extricated quite,—

And her whole beauty opens to the light.—

The bud was lovely ;—then, I could descry,

In her transition state, the leaves awry.

O perfect woman !—now, thy symmetry,

And the full fragrance of thy inmost soul,

My half-averted heart draw back to thee ;

Yielded at length unto thy just control.

Now do thy graces ravish all my breast;
And God's completed work is owned the best.
Now I thy well-adjusted beauties scan;
And for thy primal blush no longer grieve.
This is the help-meet for the perfect man—
And this the sister of the God-given Eve!

SONNET.

ON REVISITING A SPOT FAMILIAR IN YOUNGER DAYS.

ONCE more, O smallest lake ! am I reclined
Within the shadows of thy guardian trees ;
Thy shining calm, the image of the mind
With which I dreamed away in careless ease,
Again is mine.   Once more, O kindest breeze !
Forth from the slumbering depths the sparkles bring
Which ever as they meet the sun take wing,
Like brightest gems. joyous with sudden life,
And wake the waters with their fluttering dance ;
That I may start to watch the kindly strife,
And that the joy into my heart may glance.
O all ye sights and sounds, renew once more,
O play your gentle beauties o'er and o'er,
And 1 shall be a moment what I was before !

FAREWELL, ye lovely mountains, once again !
I gaze untired upon your solemn blue
With heart as full, and calmer still than when
Its depth serene at first reflected you ;
And watch, as in the boat I glide away,
Your bold, but distance-softened outline change,
As ye were stirring in an awful play,
And grandly moving to a motion strange ;
Now frowning high, yet when your pleasure wills,
Sinking behind the intervening hills.
E'en as you seem, my soul is calm,—howe'er,
Perchance a motion and a life are there,
Weaving to thought the beauteous forms I see,
Creating there a light shall one day burst on me !

DEATH OF A YOUNG GIRL.

Our meek and silent Emma then is gone !
And we are mourning over one we loved ;
Yet who could scarce be said to love in turn,
So cold and passionless and pure she seemed.
A girl of fifteen summers,—in her face
Most beautiful, in words most kind and sweet ;
Patient beneath her duty's slender calls,
And unrepining at whatever came :
But yet, a mystery, she moved about,
With no more sympathy for breathing things
Than what was needed for her being here ;
Seeking no tie but those by nature hers,
Her thoughts and her affections all unknown.
Her life brought no distress nor joy to her,
So peacefully she rested on the sea
Of measureless content. She never seemed
Like one of humankind : or, if she did,

Like one who moved and spoke, yet all the while
Dwelling serenely in a blissful dream.
We might have deemed her sinless: as it was,
She never could have wandered far from heaven.
Her heart was in her thoughts, and they, no doubt,
Were pure and beautiful in sight of God—
A sacred wedlock, in itself content—
And so she seemed to seek no love beyond.

And could they call thee *cold*, thou angel one,
Because thy spirit ne'er was bared to us;
But, like the new moon dark among the stars,
Shone to some other world, but not to this,
Save in the palest outline of her form,
Her brightness turning to the holy sky!
Or wert thou but the more the heavenly guest,
Because thy heart and soul found each their love—
The human on the breast of the divine?

How softly, too, thy spirit stole from us!
And, ere we knew it, was in heaven again!
As when a fainting breeze, unheard, yet heard,

Melts to the murmur that the ear will make
When silence reigns supreme ; we start—and lo !
The sound has faded into memory's realm.
The cords of life which tied thee were not *snapped,*
But gently drawn and made attenuate,
Until they *were not* for their subtleness !
Death came, and found thy soul already loose ;
He looked again—it seemed within thy lips,
Yet when he made the sign it moved away.

The flowers upon thy grave their petals close,
To shade their hearts from day—and so, are pale.
But at the spirit hour they ope their lids,
To catch a vision of the starry host,
And drink the light that quickens naught but soul,
And for return breathe out their balmy lives,—
Meek emblems of thy being—holy flowers !

Farewell, thou dear poetic maid ! although
The music of thy being was unheard.
As zephyrs breathing the pine-groves among,
So is thy memory lingering in the heart.

THALASSION.

A PIECE of wreck the waves did waft ashore;
  A mother and her little one it bore :
Her arm upreared the child aloft did hold,
  So that it might not touch the waters cold.
And though she felt her own life-blood to chill,
  And the benumbing pain she knew must kill;
Above her struggled still her arm, to save
  Her infant, haply, from that icy grave.
And lo ! at length the waters bore them o'er
  The place of billowy strife, and on the shore,
Beyond the ravening waves, secure from harm,
  She lay, in joy unloosing then her arm.

  She did not move; but yet through fixèd eyes
  She gazed with love upon that little prize
That she had rescued for a life she could not hope
    to share :
And there was 'neath her lids a joyful tear

That would not burst its prison-house, for fear
It might an instant cloud her view of that dear in-
     fant there.

She hopes for *life*, though knowing she must die:
But life for *him* she holdeth in her eye ;—
A hope undimmed by doubt, that fills her way
To deathly night with gladder hues of day.
Her bosom warmeth with the thought it brings;
Within her heart a gush of rapture springs;
And quite forgotten is her dying woe !
In one quick dream, the memory of the past,—
The hopeful future too, come rushing in at last ;
—The flood of feeling makes her white cold face
     to glow !

The child released, now crept along the sand ;
No longer to restrain it, could she stretch her hand.
Attracted by the breaking surf, it moved,
And held its arms that way, as to a thing it loved;
Until it reached and fell among the waves,—
And over it the greedy water raves,

And dashes to and fro the helpless thing,
With deathly grasp again its victim rescuing.

The mother moved not, when the rude waves
    killed ;
She wept not, for the fount of tears was chilled :
Yet saw she all the horror of the tale,
And felt the sword-like pang for that she could
    not wail.
And, like the trembling of the fearful oak,
Before the lightning rives it with its stroke,
A shudder ran along her silent form,
And then a groan betrayed her spirit's storm :
—A groan of death—for lo ! now all is still ;
And grief was quicker than the cold to kill.

LOVE AND ASTRONOMY.

SCENE. *A garden.*   ERNEST *and* MALFORT.

MALFORT.

COME, tell the story,—let your fullness ooze.
Where was it? What said you? And what the
    lady?
Of late you've worn a covering round your heart,
And poured the dolour of a scanty speech
In mine impatient bosom.

ERNEST.

              Now, forgive me.
I did but wait the calming of the storm
That tossed my heart about, to hoist the sails,
And glide in company with thine again.
Until the bubble of suspense had burst,
And all its shining hopes and darker doubts
Collapsed into a drop of certainty,
I could not love to speak its thousand hues.

Dawned has the future on me now; and since
The light illumes the dimness of the past,
And all about me, hopeful, sweet, and fair,
Springs up the radiant, melodious morn,
Now we'll discourse of the last and brightest scene
Of all my simple drama.

MALFORT.

Well, proceed.
I missed you and the lady yester-eve.

ERNEST.

We stole beyond the threshold to the sky,
In cloudless azure then,—by scattered stars,
And the round moon adorned.   Methought the moon
Seemed then like one who watched above her children
With the soft splendour of her steady eye.
Again,—it seemed the opening into heaven,
And that the angels in their spheres of light
Were thronging to that gate, to blend their looks
In one full gaze, and manifest their love
Unto the rapture-silenced earth.

MALFORT.

Well, well.

ERNEST.

We issued forth and moved along these paths ;
And all about us was in stillness steeped ;
And words grew fewer as we went, and felt
The eloquence of silence ;—the hushed breath
Of beauty in her most entrancing hour.
And like repose within our hearts had been,
But for a heavy thought that made them sink—
A weight too great for happy utterance,
That made its prison tremble when we spoke—
A thought, a hope, that feared to find relief.
I felt, (and so did she, as afterwards
She told me,) that the time had come at length
When we should pass beyond uncertainty,
And make belief, conviction.   Yet I felt
A choking something when I strove to speak
The word.   We wandered to the verge of this
Sweet grove, and leaning 'gainst contiguous trees,
Stood gazing at the sky.—

MALFORT.

And then?

ERNEST.

We presently conceived a sudden love
For talking of the stars.   With heartless words,
And sentences oft left unfinished quite,
And thoughts half told, and then in nonsense lost,
—To which however either would assent—
Discussed the constellations.

MALFORT.

Well, what then?

ERNEST.

We still continued speaking of the stars.

MALFORT.

I cry you mercy, Sir ! I thought you wished
To speak of love, not to investigate
The stars.   I have an almanac at home,
Containing much astronomy.   I'll lend
The book to you and Mistress Julia.

ERNEST.

Soft, Malfort—is not *Venus* in the skies?

Be patient;—*she* did tell the tale for us.

Unconsciously the lady asked the name

Of that bright star; and I as thoughtlessly

Replied, " 'Tis Venus!"—'Twas a guilty word!

And so, we both to silence sank again,

And felt each other's blushes in the dark.

But as the stillness deepened, so the pain,

The wish, and the necessity to speak.

I burst the pressure with " The star of love!—

And O! what better time than 'neath its light,—

When so auspiciously 'tis shining there,

And telling of the love it bears us both,—

Julia,—to speak my own?"

MALFORT.

                    Illustrious!

ERNEST.

Advancing as I spoke.   The chasm was leapt;

And with firm heart and foot I trod along;

And words flowed freely as a mountain stream,
Till all was said.

MALFORT.

And for the maid now, Ernest?

ERNEST.

She stood immovable beneath my words,
And silent when I ceased.   And to the plaint
Which somewhat clamourously I urged, that she
Should tell the story of *her* heart, replied
But with an eye of mild reproach.   And yet,
There dwelt in every motion, look, and word,
A sweet and cheerful trust, betraying love
As truly as man's volubility.
I've learned that woman's love is in her *heart;*
From which it radiates most equably
Through looks, and tones, and meaning acts; while man's
Is fond of revelling upon his lips.
His is the noisy and impetuous blaze;—

Now great and beautiful, then faint again ;—
And hers th' eternal heat, more felt than heard !

MALFORT.

Most right philosopher, and happy man !

ह   (−9)

MARY.

O HAPPY one! I hear thy glad voice flinging
Its cheerfulness, like sunshine, all around.
'Tis not thy voice!—it is thy heart is ringing
Its silvery peals, that joy may all abound;
And scattering the sweet contagion of the sound.

And from thy *presence* only, there is springing
A sweetness I can hear,—a ceaseless tone,
Alike that happy, universal singing
At noon of summer's day that reigns alone :—
The music of still life, when every noise hath flown.

The music of thy spirit thou didst borrow
From all the warbled strains of joyous May;
When o'er the air there floats no note of sorrow,
And sparkling songs crowd all the gloom away :—
Thou comest!—saddest hearts find welcome holiday.

As the fresh snows the mountain summits cresting,
Above the storms, are fresh for endless years;
So thou, although the cares of woman breasting,
Art young as childhood in thy hopes and fears;
Unsullied by the ills that else would bring thee tears.

The sad and weary things that make life's story,
Thy joyous warmth of soul have failed to chill.
Naught e'er can make the diamond lose its glory;
Thy nature, so, its freshness never will:
To me it seemeth ever crystallizing still!

Hast thou some harmony of heart and duty,
To us, more wayward children, quite unknown?
Hath heaven a fairer image in the beauty
Of thy fair, guiltless life, than in our own;
That joy unsleeping sits within *thy* breast alone?

SKETCH.

KAAKOUT. *

THE gentle wind, upon this odourous bank
Strewn o'er with dry birch boughs, will love to play.
My eyes, upon this fair and grassy lawn—
Half sun, half shade, so close imbowered by oaks
And chestnuts now with blossoms hoar, and fringed
With snowy alder flowers,—will find a rest.
How sweet a grove has nature planted here!
How sweet a lawn, so rich with various green!
While yet a few faint rosy spots bespeak
The latest blossoms of the eglantine:
And through the glancing leaves, tossed by the
   breeze,
The scarlet and the golden butterflies ,
Are glittering too, like living, moving flowers.
And hark! the simple song the thrush is singing;

4*

But yet so rich, so full of melody,
Heard loud and clear above these other notes.
And hark! that rustling there among the leaves,—
The startled tortoise planning an escape.
Thought is a labour to the raptured soul
Attracted by the blooming, singing earth
Beyond itself; and, thoughtless as the birds,
I long to sing with them.—But lo! the trees
Are rocking in their mossy beds; the wind,
Laden with perfume from the new-mown fields,
Is rustling in their tops; the fragrant air
Receives new fragrance from the freshened breeze;
And when the sighing ceases, robin, thrush,
And all the throng of birds pour out new joy.

SKETCH.

PLAUTERKILL.

'Tis summer's fervid night; and thick, damp clouds,
Yet lit anon by lurid flashes, swarm
About the dimness of the moonless earth.
The almost viewless, mist-hid, glimmering stars
Gleam faintly forth, and faintly disappear,
To gleam again; yet, all alive the air
With busy insect-clamour.—Hark! O hark!
A deeper sound billows the deadened air!—
The startled watch-dog barks his fierce alarm;
But through the quiet woods the sound is soft,
And echoes a low murmur to the ear,
Pervading all the heart with sense of peace.

ODE.

ON OUR NATION'S BIRTHDAY.

FORTH from the willows, where the wind
 Hath sighed its saddest note to thee;
 Where breathings of a mournful mind
Have made thy chords in unison to be;
Come, O my harp! and wake thy cheerful strings!
Make of thy gladdest song a joyous birth:
'Tis thine to listen while the spirit sings,
And echo forth the notes to all the earth.

 'Tis thine the music of the soul to hear,
 —The heaven-sent music in the poet's heart,—
 And by the wondrous magic of thine art
To make the strain be heard by every human ear.

 Come from the willows, harp!—a new, new song
Is longing on the wings of poesy to fly—
 A new, new song, both loud and long,
 Its theme, among the highest, high!

Breathe out the notes the sighing wind hath taught;
No longer with the waving willows mourn;
For lo! a joy to all the land is brought;
Th' expected beams the waiting hills adorn.
Rejoice, rejoice!—make every heart rejoice!
The sun has given the glittering hills a voice.
From east to west the glory flies away,
Till all the land is glowing in the day.

II.

The sun is glancing o'er a nation's jubilee:
    The stars have set upon another year.
    The day, the holy day again is here—
    The day on which my country first was free,
The day on which a nation it began to be;—
    And all is bright and happy yet.
    The story of the glorious past
    A million hearts are brooding o'er;
    The tale is told from first to last—
    The tale our fathers told before—
The tale—O, woe the day we ever shall forget!—

And here and there a solemn prayer
Is mounting through the blessed air ;
And all that love the land are gay,
Come forth in joy on this their country's day !

III.

The sun is mingling too *his* joy with ours,
And sending smiles upon the smiling earth.
Beneath his look the snowy clouds have birth.

The mists are mounting to the sky
To join the glorious host above :—
Upon the breast of heaven to lie
And watch us with their face of love :—
To look upon us in these joyful hours.

The gaudy fields are all in rapture resting,
The flowers are sparkling in a thousand vales,
The leaves are fluttering o'er the hills and dales,
Millions of singing things the air are breasting;
All living things breathe freer in their play
To welcome in, to bless the holy day ;—
Shame to the heart that would not then be gay !

IV.

My country! I would love thee, though
A tyrant held thee in his arms;
Though anarchy rode fiercely through,
Clad with his worst alarms.
I needs must love the mother whose warm breast
Nourished my infant life and gave my boyhood rest,
E'en though in after years she raise the rod,
 And drive me from th' embrace.
—A debt, as much a debt as that to God,
 Which nothing can efface—
And though a warmer welcome may be found
 Upon a stranger ground,
Still must the early love its vigils keep,
Far in the heart's serene and changeless deep.
 But since thy early slumbers
 Were fed with peaceful numbers,
When once the travail of thy birth was o'er;
And freedom and her sister spirits at that time
Enchanted thy young ear with many a sweet-toned
 chime,
And gave a dream more rich than land e'er dreamed
 before;

And since thy fresh, fair face
Hath yet so sweet a grace;
As yet untouched by weakening age,
Unscarred by cruelty and rage;
And since the dream hath found its counterpart
In thy rich blooming youth,
And they who love thee in their heart
Seem bowing at the throne of truth—
Who could not more than love thee, when he feels
Thy kindness, which long use almost conceals?

v.

Our fathers, who had felt
What 'twas *not* to be free,
Knew how to value their rich boon;
But we, who never knelt
To aught but liberty,
And never with unwilling hands
Perform the duty she commands,
Forget to prize her, all too soon.
Yet though our patriotic fire
To meaner things will oft give place,

And much of that pure love retire
Which fired the fathers of our race,
It is but resting in our inner heart,—
Not all expiring in the air;
And still kept warm within that holy part,
Slumbers, like unbreathed music, there.
It *shall* awake !
Whene'er occasion call,
'Twill quickly break
Its evanescent thrall,
And burst full-winged forth from its chrysalis,
Leaving its darkened home for a new state of bliss :
Shake but its crimson folds,
The flag of love will yet unfurl,
And in our hearts will proudly curl ;—
Not all extinct is Ætna's fire,
Though shoot not always forth its flames in ire.

VI.

O young and blessed land ! thy early story
Is ever for thy sons a spot of glory—
A thing to fix their eyes upon forever :
The light they live by burneth there,

5

Too bright for any falser glare
Their love from that dear spot to sever.
While there are those that on their fathers' knees
   Shall prattle of thy early days,
Still shall the flag of freedom court the breeze—
      Still may we proudly praise !

VII.

Thy rugged sons, the tillers of thy soil,
Enjoy thy bounties with a glad content ;
And in their well-rewarded toil,
Ne'er yearn for yonder sicklied continent.
Oh, where so few who never know a sigh !
" This be our home"—the universal cry.
Forever bound to such an heritage,
A love like theirs must mock the ill presage
Of those who fancy ruin is at hand
To mar the bliss that fills our native land.

VIII.

And O ! what wondrous hopes hath every one !
Such common hope will surely bind us fast.

Strongest is hope when life is just begun :
Despair ne'er springs from out so brief a past.
   And strength and wisdom, virtue too,
   With vigourous growth, go on in might.
  Our rosy dawn is scarcely through :
  Far distant is the dismal night.
  No nation e'er by poets sung
  So full of promise, when so young !
  And those of 'meditative ken
  Are sanguine as the rudest, when
  They pierce in hope thy coming years,
  And tell, with voice bereft of fears,
  Our grounds of glorious confidence.
  And *is* this universal sense,
  This common instinct, but a lie ?
  Ye prophets o'er the olden sea,
  Your croaking strains we may defy !
  That all we hope our land shall be,
  Ye more than half suspect it will,
  When with such rare and constant skill
  Ye labour, in attempt to prove
  The folly of our hopeful love !—

But O, my harp, I must not stay
To fight with fancies on a day
Like this, when every vapourous fear
Before the warmth of love must disappear.
For 'neath the sky of hope, to-day,
Contagious joys, like breezes, play.

IX.

Rejoice, O blessed land! in this thy day.
O let thy ocean-guarded shores rejoice!
And let thy plenty-swelling plains have too a voice,
That to the heart of nature melt away
Deep in the prairie-dappled, forest-crowned west.
Nor let the hills have rest!
And thy sky-dwelling peaks, where freshest snow,
Defying time, is fresh for endless years;
And where, uplifted for the stains below,
A spotless sacrifice appears—
Let *them* remember thee, and thanks, and praise,
And prayer, in holy silence raise.
And if the aspect of the beauteous earth
May teach the lesson of its birth

From God, to man's religious heart;
  O surely then, thy verdant face,—
Not covered o'er with centuries of art,
  But wild and strong, in nature's grace,—
  Is fresher with the marks of Him
  Who sits between the cherubim.
Then with the best of joy that man can give,
  To-day, O let our pæans live!

x.

  Sing—O, sing! the air is warm,
  Heated with the breath of love;
  For a million wishes swarm,
  To the mother now to prove,
  All are grateful for her care,
  All are ready with a prayer
  Now to load the willing air.
  Sing, for joy hath built her nest
  In every heart, on every tree;
  Nature is in blissful rest;
  Man is ripe for jollity.
  The gale is waiting on the shore
  To bear the sound the ocean o'er;
  5*

To all the listening lands to tell
That we love our own so well.
Then raise a swelling song through all the land,
For lo!—the blessed band,
The ones of old who made us free,
Are with us in our jubilee—
Are waiting round us now to hear
The music that their children make:
The holy ones are hovering near,
Then let our songs the stillness break!

But sleep, my harp! for now 'tis noon.
Beneath the living sun all things have rest;
And mirth must reach its zenith soon,
And sleep, in silence lost, on joy's own breast.

SONNETS.

[WRITTEN IN MARCH.]

Once more, my own surpassing one! once more,
My cares now gone, wanders my heart to thee.
With faintest bloom the spring is spreading o'er
The grave where now lies winter's sovereignty.
Light bounds the heart when fields begin to smile,
The bud of promise opening the while.
But ah! from thine image my being takes
More blissful motion than the season makes,
Thou dear, dear girl!—Between us mountains heave,
And ice-pent rivers for their freedom grieve;
The warmth that loosens them my heart sets free,
O'er plains and mountains to its home to fly.
The time is now the dawn of love to me,
With rosy hopes just mounting through the sky!

II.

Gaunt Fear with too much fear is nigh to death.
This warm south-wind a lulling burden sings.
He could but waste away when every breath
A firmer hope unto the season brings.
So, when I think of thee, and of the bliss
Begun, dear girl, on thy love-laden kiss ;
My heart is quicker than the earth to bloom !
For Hope is glowing all throughout its room,
And Love is blossoming in beauteous forms,

And Fancy in its sky beholds no storms.
Ah, what a dream is this to live within !
And what a life, if it should be no dream !
If Certainty the palm from Hope should win,
And all things *be* as bright as now they *seem!*

III.

I call thine eyes most heavenly eyes, and yet,
So well the word expresses what they are,
It is no vague and common epithet !
Of all that I could choose, the fittest far
To tell the dear compound of love and joy

Fused to the radiance with which they grace
The tender majesty of all thy face.
A word more meaning how could I employ?
Such mixture will be found in angels' eyes,
Of all the bliss which is their Being telling.
And what if to *thy* wondrous orbs does rise
The bliss that in the inner soul is dwelling!
For when their fringy curtains are unfurled,
Forever could I dream upon that heavenly world!

IV.

I heard the blackbirds piping on this morn.—
Somehow the music made me think of thee,
And stirred within my heart a sort of glee;
Though, when I issued forth, 'twas quite forlorn.
O what a power hath love! that it can make
All things subservient to its fixèd will!
For food all lovely sights and sounds can take,
The fancy and the craving heart to fill.
It is a power that love alone possesses,
One thing more beautiful than *all* to deem:
In endless loveliness that one it dresses

With hues more bright than elsewhere they would
    seem.

Thou art that blessed one, in whom *I* find

All beauty of the ocean, earth, and air combined!

EXTRACT

FROM AN UNFINISHED POEM.*

SCENE. *Upon the cliffs, overhanging a ravine.*
Night.

PHILETAS AND BOY.

PHIL.—Firm on the dusky cliffs! and motionless
As they in frozen power forever hang,

---

* This, and the two following pieces, are taken from a poem, which, in all probability, will never be completed. I have selected these, as having sufficient unity in themselves, not to depend for their interest upon that of the whole. I would not forestall criticism; yet, as the poem was not a drama, but cast in the form of soliloquy and dialogue, simply to obviate tedious narration, I may observe, that I do not claim for the words of these characters, dramatic truth; but, in making them dwell and refine upon their own emotions, have sought to give the subjective history, and the ground, of what would, in a drama, (strictly so called,) have expressed itself in other language. I allude here more particularly to the soliloquy of a man maddened by revenge, in the second and third extracts. Without saying anything of the plan or design of the whole, I would simply thus excuse myself for printing these fragments.

Let us awhile remain.   Although there be
A sound of rushing waters, still the heart
Sinks at the visible silence.   Far away
The vision floats, where placid mountains stretch
In giant slumber dimly through the night:
And nearer, heave the hills their solemn shapes
Up to the sky, that with her thousand eyes
Is watching!   What a time is this to melt
The soul into the All! Spirit of Earth!
Before whose eyes mine quaileth now, I yield
My spirit to thy clasp, to blend with thee!

And be yon moon the witness of the league;
That o'er the farthest east now looks to see
If all be ready for her holy reign;
And seeing all to adoration hushed,
And waiting, on she comes, in full-orbed sheen.
Mysterious Presence! how the sombre face
Of all things worshipping in downcast love
Brightens with sudden joy, now thou art there,—
Beneath the beams so pure and passionless!
So brighten angels' eyes, when bowed before

The Throne of thrones, His nearer presence sends
A beam of joy into their life deep bliss.
Thou eye of Heaven! I could forever meet
Thy gaze with mine, as now, did I not feel
Thy mild rebuke.   How sanctified and pure,
And fit for God alone, are all things here.
Spirit! release me from the thrall, nor hold
With beauty too intense for human hearts
My own so fixedly.   O let me range,
And freely court thee in thy thousand forms,
And be with lesser things once more at ease.
And first, and quickly, hail, thou shining river!
Lengthening and brightening with the rising moon,
And bearing up what, distant, seems a mass
Of molten gold!

Boy, *singing.*

Hark! the freshened wind is sweeping,
Round the summits of the hills:
Noiselessly it now is creeping,
Now the woods around it fills;
And over the leaves the startled snake

Glideth on to his nest in the brake;
Sharply a distant fox doth bark;
An owl doth utter a scream, but hark!—
   Hushed is every noise again,
   Lapsing to its former dream,
   Save the ear doth listen, when
   Murmureth the distant stream.

   O that it were day, that we,
   Cheerful as the mountain rills,
   Could behold their jollity,
   As they tumble from the hills;
Or clamber the crags to gather the flowers
Nursed to their beauty by delicate showers
Mounting in mist to the rocks so tall,
—The breath of the troubled waterfall.
   Sweet indeed the day, when we
   Haunt the place we love so well;
   Where the torrents sport in glee
   Through the mountain-guarded dell.

PHILETAS.

Aye, boy, I hear the torrent's softened roar,

And the faint rushing of the fluttering rills,—
Thy voice their music's herald. Everywhere
From east to west within this mountain chasm
Soundeth the stream; and ever has, since earth
From horrid chaos into order broke,
 And discords blended into music, then
First known; and through the ages has thy voice,
O stream! been echoing of that primal song.
Or if the unseen ruin from beneath,
Shattered the solid earth with pent-up breath,
Until it yawned in horror; then the springs
And rills and torrents, rushing to a mass,
Screamed through the parting crash, and thou wert
　　　born!
O that I were the spirit of thy being,
And could throughout thy sinless waters glide:
 From thy still depths up at the holy moon
 To gaze all unabashed, or broken else
 In dizzy waves, to multiply the stars;
 To ripple softly over smooth-washed stones;
 To linger near the gold-green moss, or dream
 Beneath the banks where sleep the flowers, or else

To dash in zig-zag fury down the rocks,
Or o'er some smoother, even slope to pour
In glassy silence.   O, I rush with thee
Through the curved channels thou thyself hast worn,
In blackest mass: or in exulting foam
Dart to the sudden brink, all mad with joy!
Then in the fiercest ecstacy of all—
Faint into darkness, while the trees and rocks
And mountains rise in misty grandeur up,
Like ghostly shapes, and vanish as they rise:
But lo! awakened in the frighted pool,
And from the sky in stunning thunder coming,
White as the melted moon! and O, to leap
About that radiant column in the spray,
Adorning more its beauty, then to fall
Into the groaning, quivering depths below!
And roused once more, with gathered strength again,
Far through the crevices of earth to hiss,
Until the crowded rocks shall burst!—Alas,
My solitude is broken.

FROM THE SAME POEM.

SCENE. *Another part of the Forest.*

TIMOUR.

THE forest trembleth in its deeps;
The shadowing heaven in pity weeps;
The hearts that in the lonely dell
Have beat their wonted pulses well,
Are stirring with a sudden fear;
For lo! the Avenging one is here.
The golden light that fills the skies,
So blessed to the lover's eyes,
Must blacken soon before their sight;
Their sunbright day be darkest night.
I may not stop: I will not stay,
Until the soul have passed away
Of him whom I have vowed my foe.
Hate as deep as mine, I know,
Ne'er shall lose its promised boon

6*

For all the bliss beneath the moon.

There is a pain within my breast,—

A demon clinging to my heart;

The agony can never rest,

And thence the fiend will never part,

Until the deadly deed is done;

And when the victory shall be won,

Then this raging fire shall cease,

Though I fear the after peace.

But yet the thought it will not be

Is still the fiercest misery;

And all I hope of happiness

Is born from out this dire distress.

Receive me then, ye solemn trees!

A bane to blight your holy peace.

Ye darkening clouds, grow darker still!

Revenge is brooding o'er its will.

To the fatal task I move—

Hate hath murdered sleeping love,

And, quickened to a giant life,

Is armèd now for deadly strife.

Th' Avenger speaks.—The lonely dell

Is heavy with the dismal load:
Driven by the dreadful spell
O'er the valleys he hath strode,
Sleep nor rest he hath not known,
Swift the frantic days have flown,
Till the promised spot of peace
Where the lovers hoped to dream
Now hath bid his wanderings cease—
Turned to light hope's fainter gleam.
Night is brooding o'er the hills,
Hastening e'er her time to-day;
And the distant mountain rills
Sullen drop, no more in play.
I hear them now:—Philetas, sleep,
Dream thy fill of dreams to-night—
Erasta, now prepare to weep;
Joy to thee is finished quite;
Death to-morrow rules the day,
Thy lover's soul shall pass away.
Night! thy wings are black as jet,
But paint thy pinions blacker yet!
Day! thy morning hues are red,

But stain them of a deeper dye!
Blood to-morrow must be shed,
For th' Avenging one is nigh!
Clothe the morning with a glare
That shall burn the frighted air!
Pass, O night, and haste, O day,
The lion panteth for his prey!

FROM THE SAME.

TIMOUR.

IT is the burning summer-time,
And now the sun is in his prime;
But yet the air is cool to me,
And grateful to my fevered brow;
Although, as I may plainly see,
No life is in the welkin now;
No bird, or fragment of a breeze,
Enough to touch the loftiest trees.
O, why this universal sleep!
I feel within the will to weep,
And drown with some unmanly tears
This gathering crowd of weakening fears.
I'll lose the liquid burden—then
I shall be free and strong again.
O feeble wretch! to falter here—
Arouse! for lo, the time is near!

The place, the hour have come at length,

And thou hast need of all thy strength.

He, whom so earnestly I seek,

And have, for many a weary week,

Is wandering in this very path,

And shall he now escape my wrath?

I swear by all the hate I feel

I'll freeze this fountain hard as steel,

And if I ever weep again,

Fly howling from the sight of men!

Then onward, onward do I strive,—

The only living thing alive!

Accursed be this leaden hour—

Is earth bereft of all its power?

I list, I look—but not a sound

Is ringing in the clear profound:

And not a living thing doth fly

Before me as I wander by.

I would that now a thunder peal

Athwart the lazy sky would ring:

'Twould make me strong, if I should fee

Its echo in my breast to sing.

But no, the woods are breathless still ;
I cannot wake them if I will.
To glide among them now I seem
Just like a ghost within a dream.

Boy, *singing in the distance.*

Now no more the thrasher sings
   Pensively his triple note ;
Holy mid-day ever brings
   Respite to his warbling throat.

But he hath a fainter song—
   Now it steals upon my ear,—
Soft and sweet, not over long,
   Which the good alone can hear.

I should disobey the hour,
   Sung I not my softest lay ;
He who knoweth not its power
   Let him learn it while he may.

TIMOUR.

A sound from out the distance breaks

The torpor of the time, and makes
The earth to seem alive once more.
'Tis merrier than it was before,
For as I turn these rocks around,
I catch another welcome sound.
I hear the distant waterfalls—
From sloth to life my heart it calls.
A stream is now my steps before,
And soon I'll hear its cheering roar.
And thither from the noonday heat
Mine enemy hath bent his feet;
And in the coolness of the spray
The deed of death I'll do to-day.
I creep within the shadows now—
I'd have them rest upon my brow—
The solemn groves do hem me in,
And now I speed the prize to win.
See!—they open me before,
Passing swiftly to the past;
I could never count them o'er,
They are rushing by so fast:
Now, they in the distance fade;—

Spots of sunshine in the shade,
Mossy logs and bushes low,
Boughs and branches—on they go—
Hoary rocks and aged trees
Flee like leaves before the breeze.
Earth below with berries red,
And the canopy o'erhead
Weave within the restless piece,
Which to change does never cease.
Sky of green, with golden suns,
Sky of green, with rosy stars—
Everything to madness runs,
And all lucid vision bars;
Whirling as they pass me by,
Me, the centre of the sky!

I know, by all that now I see,
There is a fever in my brain;
But that is nothing now to me,
Although to madden me 'tis fain.
When revenge hath drunk his fill,
—Sweetest drop of all to drain,

And the medicine soon that will
Cool the fever of my brain,—
Then will cease my body's thirst ;
That will cure this pain accurst.
For the pain of hate I'm sure
Death can be the only cure.
I only care to speed in this,
My all and only chance of bliss.
For I am now, where'er I go,
Least happy of all men below.
It is my doom.—I cannot cease
To seek this dread and desperate peace.
Though there be an after pain,
Worse than this it cannot be ;
So I struggle on again.—
My heart is mailed in misery !

SONNET.

O NOT alone, dear maiden, not alone

In summer groves, or by the shaded stream,

Or when the moon sent down her holiest beam,

Swift over us the bright-hued hours have flown ;—

When hand in hand we've wandered with the breeze,

And wooed the whisper of the waving trees.

As deep a love-born bliss was round us, when

We've sat together on some winter's eve,

And drank the music which the poets leave

E'en from the printed page—and then, O then !

When thou hast raised those kindling eyes of thine,

That imaged all the transport that was mine,

O in that glance was ended and begun

The sympathy that blended both our hearts in one.

VERSES

O WANDER with me, Mary, where
    The fields are fairest in the day;
And let us breathe the blessed air
Within the woods so tuneful there,
    So tuneful with the joy of May.

Deep is the azure of the sky—
    So clear and deep, as it were given
To those who look with earnest eye,
    To know the purity of heaven.

Yet will the fields of blue confess
    A brightness equal to their own;
So pure and deep the living dress,
So sweet the verdant tenderness
    O'er these our earthly fields bestrown.

It swells on many a gentle mound,
   And deepens where it finds the vale;
Yet sobers to a darker ground,
   Where over it the shadows sail.

The light is dwelling on the glass
   Of many a heaven-infolding stream;
And yet it kindles all the grass
With dearer hues, that may surpass
   The beauty in an angel's dream.

And flowers are sparkling underneath,
   And nod within the dimmer wood;
And sweeter odours than they breathe,
   Earth will not furnish if she could.

All *night* the stars look down, to lend
   Their love, to watch the sleeping flowers;
And beauty through the gloom they send
   And life upon the dewy showers.

All *day* the flowers look up, and lend
   Fragrance and beauty to the air;
And thus their meed of love they send,
   Up to the heavenly children there.

O, there are white anemone,
   And violets too, in sun and shade;
And other ones, as fair to see,
   There, their Eden-ground have made.

And on the branches far and near,
   Are birds to bless the forest haunt;
And notes, that strike upon the ear
   Like tones of silver bells, they chaunt.

Delight is everywhere supreme;
   As though, beneath such holy skies,
The world were striving now to seem,
   As much as may, like Paradise.

The clouds that lie upon the breast
   Of heaven, and cannot speak their bliss,

Send forth the soft winds from their rest,
That earth the story may not miss.

And the glad meadows and the trees
Whisper an universal word ;
And living things mount on the breeze,
Warble within the upper seas—
—The tale up in the sky is heard.

O ! one must feel, who looketh here,
His heart to sicken soon with love ;
'Tis but a wandering day, I fear,
Lost from the blessed days above.

O Mary, if the heart will feel
The joy of all without its room ;
Our bliss we never can conceal ;
But must, as do the birds, reveal
The light which doth within us steal
Upon, and chase away our gloom.

And music must be felt within—
Will find in words its proper vent,

If, in this world of stain and sin,
  To kindred hearts we may be sent.

Now, I am grateful, can I be
  A priest to minister between
That hue of heaven which now I see
Upon the grass, and on the tree,
  And which may in the heart be seen.

And when I wander far away,
  And joys unknown, and pains unknown,
Shall come to teach me what to pray;
No little bliss 'twill be to say,
That other spirits love the May
  A something more, for this mine own.

———

  O, I see a willow waving
    O'er a stream so tenderly.
  Lovingly that stream is laving
    In return that loving tree!

I behold the mountains sleeping
    All between the earth and sky.
What is this?—And am I weeping?
    Yes, a tear is in my eye!

For I know the might and madness
    Of the thundering waterfalls:
That a voice without a sadness
    In a ceaseless rapture calls.

And what are these? O Mary, in that willow,
    And in the mountains sleeping in the sky,
Are mystic dreams that haunt my nightly pillow,
    And dry, and make the tear within my eye!

They float like twilight clouds, in crimson glory,
    In hushed imagination's golden air!
The heavenly phantoms of the blessed story
    The wondrous Past doth in its bosom bear.

Dear memories! and dearer hopes! O, they
    Do make my spirit cling to what I see;

Yet I should sicken at the beauteous May,
   Were there no loving eye to look with me.

O Mary, all that now we see and feel
   Will brightly linger for the inner eye;
Will live in many a glorious shape to steal
   Upon the soul, to bless, to beautify!

Then let us drink the rapture of the morn,
   And be of all its loveliness aware.
Sensations sweet as life are yet unborn,
   That will not slumber on a day so fair.

One closing word:—this bloom of all the earth,
   Ere long, must die before the winter's breath.
As surely too, the bloom that hath its birth
   Within the heart, will one day reach its death.

But ere the beauty all shall go,
   —A withered wreath for winter made—
O, well I know, some shower of snow
Shall whiten all the air below,
   And every hue of earth shall fade.

And then shall seem the fields and skies
Pure as a lamb for sacrifice !

And ere our master, Death, shall call,
  O, may some shower of grace be given,
Upon our earthly hearts to fall,
  And make them white, and fit for heaven !

VERSES

WRITTEN WHILE LEAVING THE CATSKILL MOUNTAINS.

FAREWELL, ye blessed hills ! my lingering look
O'er the bright water and the brighter fields
Floats restlessly, and fixes on your tops,
Where in one luminous line ye touch the sky.
Ye dear, dear mountains ! how I love to gaze.
O, well I know ye are a holier thing
To look upon than all the woods and fields ;
Though they be beautiful with darkest green,
And tender tints that smile so nearer by.
For ye are clad with purer hues than they ;
Mingling your earthly with the hue of heaven.
The rose of dawn blooms first upon your tops ;
And the last flushes of the dying day
Yet linger there, when all the vale is dark.
Ye rest in golden light on many a morn,

When all the homes of men are wrapped in mist.

And on your summits spendeth many a night

All of its beauty and its purity ;

When the bright moon and all the starry world

Become the gems of your unshaded crown.

Then well ye may so proudly curve along.

Ye seem to me so like a breathing thing

Forever dwelling between earth and sky,

Whose beautiful repose so oft I've watched

And felt a living sympathy, that now,—

Vast is the vacancy your absence leaves.

And greater, for the tear that needs will start

On many a morn, because ye shall not be

To give your holy welcome to mine eye.

Methinks that I can boast of deeper joy

And grander thoughts, since I have known to live

And look upon you ; that a louder strain

Swells in my heart, caught from the ceaseless song,

The loud, glad song of your bright waterfalls.

Fair as a poet's brow, serene ye look ;

Calmer and softer than the lesser hills :

Yet O, like him, what music do ye keep ;

What endless store of beauty in your breast !

The tiny moth beside the torrent sings,

And the slight harebell gleams upon the crags.

Blithe birds are there, with notes that pierce the
    shade,

And flowers that flash in many a glade alone,

And groves as solemn as a place of prayer,

And rocks that speak the chaos of their birth,

And lakes that image perfectly the stars,

And springs that ever from the deepmost heart

Of all the mountains gush, and glide in veins

To pools and lakes to keep their mirror pure !

And streams that wind through lonely dells, below

A veil of green, and over greener moss ;

Ravines that plunge in horrid beauty down,

All guarded by a wild array of cliffs ;

And cataracts that fall in gilded spray,

And foam, and rainbows—fall to be reborn !

The winds are holiest music when they come

And nestle in your everlasting robe !

And when the great birds scream, or tempest winds

Sweep down the tottering trees and loosened rocks ;

Or when the thunder rages through the chasms,
Echoes resurge from all the wooded sides,
And ring, and multiply in chorus grand !
And O, as earth-born images that come
And rest within a poet's heart, do take
A shape more heavenly, and a purer hue;
So, too, the mists that from the spreading vales
Steal up unseen, attracted to your brow,
And there repose within the light from heaven,
Become more beautiful than words can tell !
Full well I know ye are a poet's home ;—
An image of his being, he of yours.
And I am thankful it is given to me
To linger thus about you, and to fill
My soul with all the beauty of your own.
Ah ! many a time with friends who know aright
To love you, have I gazed enwrapt ; what time
The crimson sunsets or the clearer dawn
Have softened all the terror of your look,
And made you more majestic, dark, and grand.
And many a day through glens, and aged chasms,

And o'er the solemn fir-begirded peaks,

By icy brooks, and in the cooling shade,

And everywhere about your loveliness,

We've wandered careless, happy, as the light.

And many a night have cheered your gloom with
     fires

And gleeful voices, hallowed you with prayer;

Blessing each other—blessed e'er by you!

Dear blessed days and nights! thus consecrate

To friendship, and the love of nature's soul,

And worship at the altars she has made

For love to rest on, mounting to her God!

But now away I wander; yet again

I hope to come to love you better still:

So for a season will I hush the lays

That move within my heart and long to burst

To life and being in the world of song.

A thousand thronging memories do make

Your beauty yet more beautiful to me:

And they will hallow every spot, and bathe

You in their floods of tenderness and joy.

Then hear the word, ye wondrous hills! May He
Who filled you with so deep a bliss, attend
My simple prayer, that never may the time
So saddening reach me, that it may not be
Unutterable joy to sing of you!

COME IN THE MOONLIGHT.

Come in the moonlight—come in the cold.
Snow-covered the earth,
Yet O, how inviting !
Come—O come !

Come, ye sad lovers, friends who have parted,
Lonely and desolate,
All heavy-hearted ones,
Come—O come !

Come to the beauty of frost, in the silence.
Cares may be loosened,
Loves be forgotten,—
Come—O come !

Deep is the sky ;—pearl of the morning,
Rose of the twilight,

Lost in its blueness.
Come—O come !

Look up and shudder ; see the lone moon
Like a sad cherub
Passing the clouds.
Come—O come !

Lo ! she is weeping :—tears in the heaven
Twinkle and tremble.
Tenderest sister !
Come—O come !

Keen is the air ;—keener the sparkles
Sprinkling the snow-drift,
Glancing and glittering.
Come—O come !

Look to the earth,—from earth to her sister,
See which is brightest !
Both white as the angels !
Come—O come !

Robed in the purity heaven hath sent her,
Gone are the guilt-stains—
Drowned in the holiness.
Come—O come !

Grief hath no wailing ;—Rapture is silent.
Colder and purer
Freezes the spirit !
Come—O come !

PHASES OF LOVE.

"It adds a precious seeing to the eye."

Moon nor star hath beams so bright
For the calmest, purest night,
Maiden, as those eyes of thine
For the patient blue of mine.
Now that quickened joy would move
  From those ever-radiant gates ;
Yet, withheld by softer love,
  Swimming in its prison waits.
Maiden mortal ! yet I know,
Love and joy are mingled so
In the looks that angels wear
In the holiest heavenly air.
For a moment the divine,
  Reigning o'er the human part,
Dwelleth in those eyes of thine,

Dwelleth too within thy heart.
Now so beautiful they seem,
All within thee fair I deem.
For they are not ever so
   E'en to my enraptured gaze ;
Beauteous though the living glow,
   When thou dost their curtains raise,
Ever to my loving glance.
Now there's something doth enhance
All their earthly loveliness ;
Something that the heart doth bless,
Telling of a world of bliss ;
Something far too fair for this.
Coming whence we have our birth,
Cheering all the stainèd earth
With a look that hath no stain ;
Us beguiling to remain.
Maiden, now the holy spark,
   Falling earthward, lights on thee !
Though those orbs are never dark,
   Now from earthly light they're free.
Now I needs must worship thee,
Yet 'tis not idolatry !

II.

Let me rest upon my oar,
  While the trebly-sacred she
Music's dearest breath will pour
  On the evening air for me.

Though the shadows be not nigh,
  And, above the trembling tide,
Seem I floating on the sky,
  And among the stars to glide;

I have neither eye nor ear
  But for her who sits and sings.
Time, that I the most may hear,
  Flies with but a fairy's wings.

What the sound may be to some,
  I will neither say nor think.
If the spirits near us come,
  Let them all the sweetness drink.

Let the notes to yonder hill
  Pass, and sink within the trees;

And the echoes, if they will,
  Faint on the returning breeze.

Let the dear vibration kiss
  All the ripples of the stream ;
Till the water, of the bliss
  Air may bring to her, shall dream.

Sweetness such as this I've found
  Ne'er before from lips to rise.
'Tis the very soul of sound,
  Singing in her Paradise !

All the heart-born emphasis
  Words may ever have, I ween,
Is not full enough for this ;
  Aught so sweet as this to mean.

Love doth every note distil
  To the purest of its tone.
Love hath such a master skill,
  I am not amiss to own.

Love doth every sense unite.
  Nothing but the sound can be.
And the pulses of delight
  Beat in quiet ecstacy.

Maiden, Love is not a lie,
  When he blesses so thy breath.
Music without love would sigh,
  Till it sighed away to death.

Only in this rarest hour,
  When absorbing Love is here,
Music hath its proper power—
  Born of love for loving ear.

Sweet is music, sweeter still
  Love, when both the purest be.
Maiden, love thee then I will.
  Bliss they bring when they agree.

III.

The flowers are waving o'er the grass
  As gently as a rocking cloud;

9

A brilliant throng !—yet who doth pass—
A brighter thing than all the crowd ?
'Tis my beloved one !
The motion dies on every flower,
And grace abandons all the green ;
Abashed they stand, before the pow'r
Of her, the softly-gliding queen ;
They are so far outdone !

I may not say but majesty
Augustly moves before the storm ;
But in the motion springing free,
And living in the maiden's form,
I see it plainer still.
I know not but a wheaten sheaf
Droops with a quite unrivalled grace ;
But when the maiden plucks a leaf,
Her bended arms and bending face
Betray a greater skill.

She starts—as does a bounding hare,
Or like a glancing gleam ;

And on the soft up-bearing air
　Her 'wildered tresses stream
　　　As willows to the breeze !
The spirit of the laughing morn
　Impels to motion quicker far.
Possessed with joy thus newly born,
　She glides, like a departing star,
　　　Behind the dusky trees.

And I may say, now she's away,
　Did ever living thing before,
That wingeth through the heavenly blue,
　Or treads upon this earthly floor,
　　　One half so sweetly move ?
For at the sight, such dear delight
　Flits round my brain on wings of grace ;
I stand amazed, where late I gazed,
　In wonder rooted to the place ;
　　　And I am lost in love !

On many a morning's loveliness
　With weary eye we gaze about ;

But should its rising lustre bless
　　The kindling heart, I cannot doubt
　　　I am not then deceived.
And maiden, when thy graceful glee
　　So sweetly makes my heart to sigh ;
Although with looks of love I see,
　　It is no dream :—love clears the eye:
　　　Such truth must be believed.

IV.

　　Love's a-dying,
　　Not espying
Food in every look or tone ;
　　Doubts are springing,
　　Fears are ringing ;
Thus I sit and sing alone.

　　Lost in sadness,
　　Foe to gladness,
What shall bring me peace again ?
　　Day is brightening,
　　Cares are lightening ;
But it may not ease the pain.

Music hither,
Music thither,
Would seduce me not to grieve :—
Sweetest guerdon !
Hark ! the burden
Fancy cannot help but weave.

'Fishes are sporting
' All in the blue seas ;
' And insects are courting
' The glee-giving breeze ;

' The birds are all singing
' With music to cloy ;
' And flowers are swinging
' Their bright heads for joy ;

' And men are all quaffing
' The draught of to-day ;
' And maidens are laughing
' Like zephyrs in May :—
9*

'Come away from gloomy thinking,
'Be thy soul the rapture drinking ;
        'Come away !'

No, I will not ;
Grief will kill not ;
Let my sorrow take its course.
Love is sighing,
Love's a-drying
At his true and only source.

Lo ! my love is coming—
    Sorrow makes a din ;
Joy begins a humming ;
    May he enter in ?

See her eye is warming,
    And her voice is sweet :—
Love again is storming
    All my heart complete.

Oh my former blindness !
Fool was I to grieve ;
Such a look of kindness
Cannot but relieve.

Such a tone entices
Me to life again ;
And the whole suffices
Quite to kill the pain.

Bliss that I was losing
Flutters back again ;
Sweeter for refusing,
Dearer for my pain.

Love that reassureth
Cannot fail to please ;
Love it is that cureth
E'en his own disease.

Love's an air the clearest
Mortal eye may need :

Beauty then is dearest
   Loving heart to feed.

Love's an air the purest
   Mortal men can breathe :
Joy it brings is surest
   All the sky beneath,

I SEE thy arms about it prest—
   Thy gentle motion to and fro,
Thy look, that cannot be expressed,
Upon the baby at thy breast
   Betray a love I may not know.

And sure, thy love could not be less
   For *her* whose loss we now deplore;
For love she gave, in turn to bless,
And words that might relieve distress:
   She was thy child, yet something more.

I would not bid thee dry a tear,
   Nor strive to kill the rising grief
For one that was, I know, so dear,
And dearer, when no longer here;
   Nor hope to find too quick relief.

For when the cheerful airs of spring
   Shall come, upon some lovely day,
About her shaded grave to sing,
And make *to live* a blessed thing;
   Thou need'st must weep that she's away.

And ever, when the happiness
   Of life upon thy heart shall fall,
The harder touch of bitterness
Will follow then its soft caress,
   That *she's* not here to feel it all.

But haply, when thy heavier day
   Shall come, as often come it must;
And life shall seem a weary play,
Too sad to make us wish to stay;
   Thou may'st be glad she's in the dust.

I would, to love us she had staid:
   Yet, thinking how her spirit grew,
And where her treasure she had laid,
And that her home in Christ she made,

Myself I cannot but upbraid.
I judge it is the same with you.

But we are human, and to dream
Of what she *may be* in the skies,
Cannot be kept a thought supreme ;
Can never be so dear a theme
As what she *was* before our eyes.

And while her image still is near,
Not dim, till years shall wander by ;
If we should think of her, the dear,
The blooming one who left us here,
It will not harm us if we sigh.

TO MY FRIEND L. L. N.

AN EPISTLE.*

FRIEND of my heart! no longer do we live
As once, convolving in each other's life;
But in our separate orbits must we roll,
Each to the other like a lonely star
Shining away in its own realm of peace.
That was a glorious world we once created,
—The incomparable story of the past—
And by imagination lifted up
Above us, and apart, with double lustre shining,
More glorious seems than mine, or thine alone!
I fix mine eyes upon that life of love,
Now while I desultory music breathe

---

* These verses were part of a letter written while the author was re-
siding in the western part of North Carolina, a few miles east of the Blue
Ridge, to a friend then dwelling in the low country at the extreme
east of that State:—a successful invitation, as it proved, to come and
enjoy the surpassing beauty of that mountainous region.

Beneath the wind that from the mountains comes,
Flitting from top to top of every hill,
And sinks upon the branches in the vale.

Where is *thy* harp, O friend ! whose strains whilome
Were sweet as those of her " the swan" that piped
Her midnight music in thy Huron land,
Her angel whispers in the far-off sky ;
Whose tones were powerful as her clarion notes
That pierced the dark and solemn wilderness ?
O strike its golden strings again, and tell
To other lands how strong is Poesy
At the fresh bosom nursed of this our own ;
And though a feebler child, yet shall I be
Strong in my brother's strength, in thine, dear friend !
Haply, within that dismal country, where
For duty's sake thou art content to be ;
Where not a hill above the even trees
Rearing a prouder brow, is there to give
The cheerful signal of the rising sun ;
Where streams undimpled saunter by, and where
The long moss sweeping sadly, sighs forever :—
10

Thy heart is weary of thy loneliness,

And of that mournful land that ne'er is gay,

Even when nature with her fullest hand

Covers the land with golden flowers,* and fills

The air with fragrance, 'till the sense is steeped

In one sweet, sunny, sad and silent dream ;

And so thy fancy wanders.   Such food is denied

As when, blest in the full reality,—

Th' excelling presence of our dearest dreams,—

We lived to look, to listen, and to feel,

And all the while to love, in our far home

By the blue mountains.†   Such a glorious burst

Of dim sensations, thoughts sublime, and joy,

May not surprise thee now, as when we went,

The total day, thridding the thickets close,

Or up the cool and moss-adornèd path

Of the gay rill,—our own "Sweet WaterBrook,"—

Or through the clearer vista of the wood,

Forever looking upward for the spot

---

* The yellow jessamine.

† An allusion to a previous summer spent among the Catskill moun-
tains.

Of light that should proclaim our journey done,
Until at length the topmost crag shone forth,
And with a quick, ecstatic shout we rose
Once more into the region of the sky,
And felt the freedom of the purer air.
Then how the mountains rolled in hugest seas
Up to our very feet ;—blue as a crystal lake
Upon the verge of night reflecting heaven.
Then, while we looked upon the plain, where life
And motion slept, there came a something up
Inaudible, but yet most like a sound,
That quieted the blood, and made the soul
Droop at the presence of a mystery :
And as the evening deepened, and the moon
Broke o'er the distance, and around, above,
The glittering tumult of the noiseless stars
Came out upon the surface of the dark—
Then, friend ! into our open hearts came down
The full reward, and in each other's face
We saw a soul subdued by Beauty's power,
Made humble by the near approach of God.

But such a day, but one of many days,

Comes not to thee, comes not to me, *alone.*

Then would'st thou know such wondrous life
again?

Come, O come hither!—see the spots of green,

Sign of the convalescing earth, are here,

Full soon to vanquish every paler hue.

The opening willow-buds embrace the breeze,

And as they fan the tender sward beneath

Make other than their rattling winter sound,—

A soft faint promise of their summer sigh.

Hope everywhere is feeling forth again.

And, but through yonder coppice mount, and lo!

A wall of mountains girdles in the world!

Behind them is a garden of Delight,

Where sights and sounds, so beautiful, so sweet,

Vie with each other which may tell the best

The bliss that fills the air, and bathes the land.

There may we breathe intoxicating air,

And with ecstatic wonder climb the peaks

Whose very summits glow with crimson flowers

Spread in vast masses o'er the mounds of green.*

Then come, and be no more companionless!

See, how the words come trooping from my heart,

And stand arrayed to fetch thee!—O my friend!

Ne'er let us falter in the holy task

Of telling to the world that Jesus died!

Nor fail to warn, to strengthen,—ne'er forget

That we are men hung between heaven and earth,

God's bread to hand unto his feeding souls.

But when the heart is sick, and needs its balm,

Then let us meet for friendship's sacred rite.

This tyrant absence is affection's *night:*—

Glorious in holy beauty and repose,

But not so bright, so joyful as the day.

Upon the wonder of the past we feed,

Or through the future send our dreaming hopes,

When absence, like the universal dark,

---

* The summits of the Roan Mountain, in Yancey County, North
Carolina, (one of the highest of the Appalachian Range,) are a succes-
sion of "balds" or grassy eminences, stretching some nine miles
through the sky; which at the season of the *rhododendron maximum* are
covered with those flowers, in a magnificent profusion, unequalled, per-
haps, in our whole country.

Within her stubborn mantle cloaks our friend.
Then let us love the *day*, and put astir
Our hearts to welcome in its cheerful morn.
I cannot live without thee—no, my friend!
Not while I burn with all the flush of youth.
It may be, should we come to silver hairs,
And think of that last step upon the earth
Whence we shall spring above these sullen doubts,
And rise clear-visioned, disembodied, free,—
Free as the thoughts that in a twinkle shoot
Beyond the stars, that circle round the world,—
That we may be content to wait awhile,
And be apart, until the great release
All hindrances to love shall sweep away,
And we are *one* forever, and in Him,
The universal Friend, Creator, God!

GETHSEMANE.

The Saviour bowed.—"O God, if it may be,
This cup—I pray thee let it pass from me."
—The tones, they were the tones of agony.

The Perfect One, unshaken at the hour
When the strong tempter pressed with all his power,
Quailed in amazement when this cloud did lower.

"O ye of little faith"—He once did cry,
When through the dark the storm was sweeping by:
One storm there was that he could not defy.

A storm of dreary anguish gushing in;
More dreadful than the elemental din:
He sank, yet it was weakness;—'twas no sin.

Where was the Godhead, when the bloody dew
Burned on the brow of Him who died for you?
The lowly man—the great Redeemer too!

The Word who spake, and sky, and land, and sea
Became this beautiful reality:
Eternal Son of God!—yet this was He!

Ah, well we know, because He wept and prayed
When on Him thus the vast affliction weighed,
How perfectly He was our brother made.

The torture streamed through every burning vein,
Prophetic of that piercing final pain:
What wonder then the crimson drops did rain!

He took the flesh, and felt the mortal throe;
And knew the weakness that is ours below:—
To aid Him, down there must an angel go.

Not long in feebleness He lingered there;
His finished words,—the life of every prayer,—
Breathed His true strength unto the waiting air.

"But yet, O Father!—not my will, but thine."—
Of His release the Father gave no sign:
Then to the doom Himself He did resign.

And forth He stood, in calm, majestic might;
Forcing the darkness from His purer sight:
As when the day rolls back the robe of night.

And the next footfalls of that Dearest One
Betrayed the triumph that was now begun;
His body bore to death;—and all was done.

O bend thine eyes on Him the Crucified!
Clasp Him forever to thy trembling side,
Breathe in the life of Him revivified!

Hark to the wind arousing from its lair!
It comes—it screams—it dies in other air—
It goes—to find unearthly echoes,—where?

Thus will the Spirit beat upon thine own,
Feel forth to find and fasten Him alone;
Mingled with Him, sink at the Father's throne!

But lest from Him thou faltering fall away,
Loosening the blessed union in a day;
Think of Gethsemane, and watch, and pray.

WAVES BY MOONLIGHT.

HERE is another of those wondrous nights
When the soft radiance of the bright full moon
Falls gently as the snow in wintry showers
Upon the silent river, fields, and hills.
O'er the fair water swims the steady boat;
And all the distant, dusky shores along,
Her waves roll up and break in silver fire,
Which mingles, and unmingles, then dies out,
Just as another line of light is born,
And shoots along the dimness to succeed:
Eager as summer insects, full to fill
Its brief duration with a joy intense.
So, men have said, live fairies, gnomes, and sylphs,
All spirits of the elements, a life outspread
Through longer time, of pleasure waning never.
They die, as do the sparkles on the shore;
But all between the birth and death is bliss.
So, in a higher joy perpetual,

Live on the angels,—lives whose precious flow

Is varied as the aspect of the waves;

Now sweetly tranquil, as yon pure fire gliding;

Now breaking into pulses of delight.

So is not this dear beauty of the wave

Of *our* existence symbol,—lone mankind!

We roll in darkness to the shores of Death—

Waves rarely crested with the foam of joy;

But seldom living in the glow of bliss.

But cheerful—cheerful—brother of the Lord

Of angels!—when within the dazzling light

Rolling in billows from th' effulgent Throne,

Thou shalt wake up, thou wilt be glad to know

Thou wert allowed—amid the dreary gloom,

Tremblingly tossing onward to thy home—

Even by thy own constancy to win

Some faint deserving of the shadeless glory

In which at length thy soul shall bathe forever!

CPSIA information can be obtained
at www.ICGtesting.com
Printed in the USA
BVHW04*1108170918
527708BV00014B/1743/P